LORD MU

The Power of

Dedicated to my Family and Teachers

Shanthi Deepti

First Edition – September, 2017

The main Category of the book – Mythology

Mail ID: shanthi.deepthi22@gmail.com

Please like us at:-
Facebook: Shanthi Deepti
Twitter: @Shanthi Deepti

Preface

Kumara Gana Nadambha, Thushti, Pushti, Mathi, Dhrithi

Meaning: Goddess Lalitha Tripura Sundari is the mother of Murugan and Ganesha. She is personification of happiness, health, wisdom and courage.

(442nd name in LalithaSahasranamam)

Preface

Murugan is known with various names across various parts of Asia. In Tamil Nadu, Sri Lanka, Mauritius, Indonesia, Malaysia and Singapore, he is famously known as Murugan. In Kerala and Karnataka, he is famously known as Subramanyam. In North India, he is famously known as Karthik or Skanda. Born for a reason and raised to the level of Commander-in-Chief of the army of Gods. In Bhagavad Gita (v10-24), Krishna explains Arjuna about his omnipresence saying "Among generals, I am Skanda, the lord of war."

Lord Murugan is most popularly worshipped in South India and parts of Singapore. This is perhaps because Murugan spent most of his time in places in and around Tamil Nadu of India. Also many poets from South adored and wrote numerous poems on Murugan. Many of the major events in Murugan's life took place when he was a young boy. This has encouraged the worship of Murugan as a child god, very similar to the worship of the child Krishna in North India. His worship in North India might have declined after the fall of Hindu kings in the North which later was mostly ruled by Mughlas and British Empire. No matter what, people are familiar with the name Skanda and worship him as God of war.

As time passed, Murugan's importance lost with time as people later started accepting the concept of Trimurthy (Brahma, Vishnu and Shiva). This book is a small effort to bring back the lost glory of Lord Murugan. His grace on his disciples is expressed in various chapters of this book. There are various tales related to a particular incident in the story. The most appropriate ones are mentioned in this book.

1. Reason behind the birth of Lord Murugan

Long ago there lived a demon called Tarakasura. Being a demon he was more inclined to evil deeds. He along with his elder brothers Surapadma and Simhamukha started tormenting the sages and innocent people. Soon Tarakasura got control of earth and wanted to get control of heavenly worlds which was ruled by Gods. In order to fight Gods, Tarakasura felt he must be extraordinarily powerful. To achieve this, he performed severe penance to impress Lord Brahma and acquire boons. Several years passed, but no sign of Lord Brahma showing his grace on Tarakasura. So, Tarakasura intensified his penance by standing on thumb of his foot, later he stood by his head on ground and feet facing the sky and continued the penance. Huge flames fumed from Tarakasura's penance. As these flames were consuming the forests and its dwellings on earth, Lord Brahma appeared to Tarakasura.

Lord Brahma asked Tarakasura to stop his penance and ask for the boon he wanted to acquire by performing the penance. Tarakasura was waiting for this moment and asked Brahma to grant him a boon that he should be invincible and have to be killed only by the son of Lord Shiva. Lord Brahma granted the boon and disappeared.

So this was the reason why Murugan was destined to be born as son of Lord Shiva. The main purpose of his existence is to kill Tarakasura and his brothers to save the world from evil deeds of Tarakasura.

2. Sacrifice of Love

Tarakasura was wise enough in choosing the boon. Lord Shiva was in deep meditation during that period because he could not bear the separation from his wife Sati, who immolated herself. Sati took this extreme step when her father Daksha insulted her husband, Lord Shiva. Taking this situation as an advantage, Tarakasura thought Lord Shiva cannot have anymore children and requested Brahma to grant the boon. But fate had something different for Tarakasura. Sati was later born as Parvati to King Himavan and she wished to marry only Lord Shiva.

With new boon, Tarakasura and his brothers started tormenting and chasing gods from heaven. Tarakasura plundered all their valuables. He destroyed the hermitages and killed sages who offered prayers to gods. All living creatures and gods started fearing him and lived in hideouts. Unable to tolerate Tarakasura anymore, all the gods went to lord Brahma for solution as his boons to Tarakasura bought more pain to them.

Lord Brahma, who was aware of Tarakasura's misdeeds, expressed his concern and helplessness in saving gods. But he suggested that if gods can make Lord Shiva come out of his meditation and marry Parvati, a child born to them can kill Tarakasura and free gods and human beings from the misdeeds of Tarakasura. Getting little comfort from Brahma's word, gods sketched a plan to make Lord Shiva come out of his meditation and marry Parvati. To accomplish this task, gods nominated Manmadha, the god of love.

One beautiful day when Lord Shiva was in deep meditation, Manmadha created a very beautiful and pleasant environment around him adorned with fragrant flowers and beautiful waterfalls. Paravti, who wished to marry Lord Shiva, took permission from her parents and was serving him with full devotion. She was performing very difficult austerities to win the heart of Lord Shiva. Taking this as an opportunity, Manmadha released his flower arrows standing behind Lord Shiva. These flower arrows have power to develop love among the person whom they pierce and the person who stood infront of them. But Lord Shiva is beyond the magic of arrows. The arrows could not harm Lord Shiva but gave a gentle touch to him which was enough to wake Lord Shiva from his meditation.

Lord Shiva burning Manmadha and gods watching them

Lord Shiva opened his eyes in furious. In front, he found a lady worshipping him. With his vision he came to know that it was Manmadha who stuck him with arrows from behind. Lord Shiva turned to Manmadha who was hiding behind the trees and burnt him to ashes with his third eye as he disturbed his meditation. Looking back to the lady, Lord Shiva knew it was Parvati who was ever devoted to him. Her devotion and selfless service won the heart of Lord Shiva. He promised to marry Parvati as she wished.

Later as requested by Rati, wife of Manmadha, the god of love was brought back to life by Lord Shiva. But he is only visible to Rati. Since then one cannot see Manmadha but can feel the affect of his arrows. Thus with the sacrifice of god of love, Lord Shiva married Parvati. A child born with their union would kill the demon Tarakasura and his brothers.

3. Birth of Lord Murugan

Though Manmadha lost his physical body, his sacrifice pleased gods as now Lord Shiva is out of his meditation and promised to marry Parvati. On an auspicious day Lord Siva married Parvati in the presence of holy sages. Lord Shiva created a private palace for his new bride in Mount Kailash. They started living happily in their private chambers.

Several years passed and there was no news about a child being born to the divine couple. The gods can no more bear the torment caused by Tarakasura and his brothers. They again went to Lord Brahma for help as they feared to disturb the divine couple. Lord Brahma listened to the gods silently. He felt if they could impress Lord Shiva with their prayers, the ever graceful Lord would fulfill the desires of his devotees. Thinking so, all the gods along with Brahma left to Mount Kailash and started praying the divine couple infront of their private palace.

During this period, Lord Shiva and Parvati were enjoying their union. The time has come to eject the brilliance (semen) of Lord Shiva into the womb of Parvati. But this was interrupted by the prayers of gods. The semen which was bright golden yellow in color fell on earth. It was emitting fire like fumes and was consuming everything on earth. The goddess of earth could not bear the semen and requested Agni, god of fire to take this from her.

Agni took the brilliant semen into him. Meanwhile, Parvati got angry on gods who disturbed her union with Lord Shiva by which she cannot conceive. As she cannot give birth to a child, Parvati cursed gods that they cannot have children from their wives. (So the count of Hindu gods stopped at 33 crores). As goddess earth accepted her husband's semen, Parvati cursed earth that she would be wife to many men. (It is believed that every king who owns and rules his kingdom is considered as husband to goddess earth). Parvati also cursed Agni that he would eat unclean things and have unbearable inflammation all over his body for bearing the semen.

Immediately Agni started feeling inflammation all over his body and was not able to bear this. He apologized and requested the divine couple to cure his curse. Lord Shiva told Agni that he can relive from inflammation when he transfers the semen into the womb of a woman who can bear it. Immediately Agni started searching for suitable woman. In Himalayas, he found six Kritika* sisters who were shivering from cold. Agni transferred the brilliance of semen into six Kritikas so that they can bear the semen within their wombs. As the semen was divine, the Kritikas became pregnant immediately. When the Kritikas husbands knew about their pregnancy, they cursed the Kritikas to become stars in a constellation in the sky. Later the stars were famously known as Kritika nakshatra or Pleiades.

Before becoming stars the Kritikas placed their fetuses on the bank of river Ganga.

Six babies from six Kritikas

Ganga carried these fetuses in its water for years and was nurturing the fetuses. On an auspicious day, six babies were born from the fetuses. Lord Shiva and Parvati visited the place called Sarva Vana where their children were born. When Parvati took the six children into her arms, the babies united to form one body having six heads. Thus a beautiful young boy was born who would annihilate the cruel demons and become Commander-in-chief of gods.

The boy is called Skanda meaning 'spilling' as he was born out of spilling of semen. He is called as Karthik or Murugan as he was breast fed by Kritikas. He is called as Shanmukha meaning six faced. He is called as Sarvana because he was born in a place named Sarva Vana on the banks of river Ganga.

There are various stories related to the birth of Murugan based on various puranas like Skanda Purana, Shiva Purana, etc. A slight variation in the story where Murugan is born out of six flames that emerged from Lord Shiva's third eye which Agni consumes. Murugan was born to Lord Shiva to kill Tarakasura that fulfills Brahma's boon. All the gods rejoiced with the birth of Murugan and left to their abodes happily.

(Many may wonder that Ganesha, known to be the son of Lord Shiva and who is elder to Murugan could have killed Tarakasura. But Ganesha was born by mere will of Parvati who put life into the turmeric power that she dropped from her body. Ganesha was not born with union of Lord Shiva and Parvathi, so Ganesha does not fit the boon of Brahma in killing Tarakasura).

4. Commander-in-chief

With the birth of Murugan, the gods were happy. As the new born was very young, the gods gave protection to the baby. The boy had divine qualities in him. Unlike other babies, he grew faster and stronger. He had charming face and handsome looks. He showed interest in learning usage of various weapons and different techniques of warfare. Lord Shiva and Parvati were very impressed and enjoyed watching the skills of their younger son. When Murugan excelled all kinds of warfare, Lord Shiva thought to coronate the young boy as Commander-in-chief for god's army.

On an auspicious day, Lord Shiva coronated Murugan as Commander-in-chief of god's army. Various gods gifted Murugan with various powerful weapons and armours that would help him in future battles. Parvati presented the divine Vel or Spear that possesses her universal power. Kubera provided ten lakhs of his Yaksha army. Agni gave his radiance. Vayu gave a chariot that would travel as fast as wind. All gods showered blessings on the young warrior. In return, Murugan requested gods as how can he help them.

The gods who lost their heavenly city Amaravati to
demons, explained the grief that they were facing
because of Tarakasura and his brothers. The gods
were tiered living in hiding for several years.
Murugan took no time to declare war against the
cruel demons for all the trouble they were causing.
With the permission and blessings from his parents,
Murugan stood in front of god's army and marched
towards the demons entourage.

5. Killing of Tarakasura

The god's army started from Mount Kailash and marched towards its foothills. The demons heard loud sounds of drums and conches. From far they can see the flags and chariots of gods with thousands of god's army marching towards them. What surprised them the most was the scene that a young boy leading the entire army. Immediately the demons rushed to Amaravati where Tarakasura was ruling and informed about the attack from gods.

Tarakasura could not believe what the demon messenger said as there was no god who could defeat him. He ridiculously asked who dared to lead the god's army. The answer came as a young boy riding a chariot driven by horses. Listening to this, Tarakasura laughed loudly imagining the situation of gods who are now led by a young boy. Meanwhile, one of his ministers informed Tarakasura that the young boy was none but the son of Lord Shiva. Hearing this, Tarakasura felt as if he was stuck with a thunderbolt. He immediately ordered his troops for war preparations, still wondering and recovering from what he heard about the young boy.

Both the armies of gods and demons were on either side of each other. For the first time Tarakasura got complete glance of the young boy. Before the war starts Murugan gave a chance to Tarakasura to surrender and give up all his evil deeds. But Tarakasura who was full for demonic character, laughed and made fun of Murugan. He felt it was an insult for him to fight a young boy and he first ordered his ministers to destroy the god's army. A fierce battle started between the two armies. With Murugan as new Commander-in-chief, there was a healthy spirit in god's army. Indra killed most of the demons under the leadership of Murugan. Seeing the advancements of Indra, Tarakasura attacked him. Soon Indra was defeated by Tarakasura.

Murugan who created panic in the hearts of demons, killed most of the cruel demons. In his fierce form, his six faces helped him look in every direction. His 12 arms brought worst death to many demons. Tarakasura suffered huge causalities in his army because of Murugan's wrath. Now fear started filling Tarakasura's mind. He started believing that the young boy was son of Lord Shiva and had come to annihilate him. He now came face to face with Murugan. They used various divine weapons against each other. With his death standing infront of him, Tarakasura was losing the battle. Murugan finally threw his spear on Tarakasura which pierced through Tarakasura's heart. This marked the end of a wicked demon Tarakasura, fulfilling the purpose of Murugan's birth. All the gods hailed their Commander-in-chief. Since then he was also called as Mahasena meaning Captain.

6. Annihilation of Simhamukha and Surapadma

Hearing the news of Tarakasura's death by a young god, his older brothers Surapadma and Simhamukha were very furious. They decided to avenge his brother's death and waged a war against god's army.

Soon a battle was declared among the gods and demons again. As usual, Murugan gave chance for the demon brothers to surrender. Because of the demonic nature like Tarakasura, they refused to surrender. A fierce battle started. Under the leadership of Murugan, gods defeated most of the demon's army. Murugan defeated Simhamukha, the lion faced brother of Surapadma.

Surapadma heard the news of his brother's defeat. Still possessed by evil thoughts, Surapadma would not surrender and continue the battle with Murugan. Surapadma and Murugan fought with various divine and powerful weapons. In the fight Surapadma was wounded very badly with the blows of Murugan's spear. Not able to take any more suffering, Surapadma transformed himself into a big tree. Murugan found Surapadma in the guise of a tree and finally threw his spear onto the tree splitting it into two. The badly wounded Surapadma emerged from the center of the split tree and pleaded Murugan to spare his life.

Till now the demons witnessed the most horrific form of Murugan. After Simhamukha and Surapadma realized their guilty, Murugan showed mercy on the demon brothers and assured that he would protect them. He instructed the lion faced Simhamukha to become the vehicle for his mother, Parvati. As Surapadma was split into two halves of a tree, one half of the tree was instructed to become the Peacock, the vehicle for Murugan. The other half of the tree was instructed to take the form of a cock and always reside on the flag of Murugan.

Murugan is considered as a fierce warrior. This is because when evil and demonic characters dominate us, he would remove them in the form of punishment which would appear as fierce for us. But he is always compassionate and ever merciful when we surrender our ego at his feet.

7. Gift of Victory

After winning the war against the wicked demons, Indra was restored back as king of heavens. Since Indra got back his glory with the help of Murugan, he wished to gift his daughter Devasena, in marriage to Murugan. The marriage of Murugan and Devasena happened in the heaven with the blessings of gods and sages.

Lord Murugan marrying Devasena

Story of Devasena

Devasena and Daityasena were actually daughters of Prajapati Daksha. As the name indicates Devasena used to take the form of army of gods during war. Similarly Daityasena took the form of army of demons during war. Once the sisters were sporting the beauty of Himalayan mountains. A demon king by name Keshi happened to come across the sisters. He expressed his wish to carry the sisters to his kingdom for his pleasure. Daityasena who is inclined to demonic nature, liked the proposal of Keshi. But Devasena rejected the proposal. Keshi took the sisters by force and held Devasena captive.

Indra was then wandering in Himalayas for the search of able Commander-in-chief to lead his army and help in regaining his lost kingdom. He came across Devasena who was crying in agony in the captive of Keshi. Indra fought with Keshi and rescued Devasena. Alone now, Devasena was frightened and requested Indra to shelter her and find a right match who can protect her. Indra accepted Devasena as his daughter and promised to find a right match for her.

As Indra do not possess any abode, Devasena was sheltered at Lord Brahma's abode by Indra as she would be safe there. Indra requested Brahma to help him find a right match for Devasena. Brahma with his vision instructed that the child born of fire would marry her. Murugan was born from Lord Shiva's spilling which was emanating fire and also demi-god Agni sheltered the brilliance of Lord Shiva. So, Murugan was considered as right match for

Devasena. During the war with Taraksura, Indra took the help of Devasena in forming the army of gods.

8. Knowledge meeting Valour

Lord Shiva and Parvati were enjoying the feats of Murugan. During this period their elder son, Ganesha was away from Mount Kailash, doing penance to obtain Knowledge and Siddhi (enlightenment). So he was not aware of Murugan's birth. After completing his penance, he returned back to Mount Kailash and saw a young boy practicing with sharp and blunt swords. The boy looked very handsome. As the boy practiced with his 12 arms, Ganesha stood amazed watching such a feat practiced by a young boy. He wondered who the young boy could be and what was he doing near his parents private place. As Ganesha continued to walk to meet his parents, Murugan's eyes fell on Ganesha. He started wondering about the divine personality with elephant head. They both introduced themselves as son of Lord Shiva and Parvati, unaware about each other's births.

Both the sons of the divine couple went to meet their parents. It was great delight for the divine couple to watch both their sons walking together towards them. Elder son Ganesha is an embodiment of Knowledge and the younger son Murugan is embodiment of Power and Valour. Upon enquired by Ganesha and Murugan, the divine couple narrated their birth stories. Now the two sons understood that they are indeed brothers. They happily hugged each other. Since then together they were part of many adventures.

Thus the ocean of Knowledge was united with ocean of Valour. Though Ganesha and Murugan appear as two different deities, devotees who worship either Ganesha or Murugan would be blessed with both Knowledge and Valour (Courage) as they both are inseparable brothers.

9. Leaving the place of Salvation

Years passed by watching the skills and abilities of their sons by the divine couple in Mount Kailash. At times they test their son's knowledge and valour by conducting some tests and plays with them. One day the divine couple set a test for Ganesha and Murugan. The parents asked them to circle the world three times and who came back first would be the winner and will be rewarded with a prize. (Some stories mention that the prize was a fruit given by Sage Narada to the divine couple. The fruit should be given to the person whom they liked the most).

Hearing the words of Lord Shiva and Parvati, Murugan immediately mounted his Peacock vehicle to circle round the world. On the other hand Ganesha stood still. He thought for a while. Then he prostrated to Lord Shiva and Parvati and started to circumambulate (moving around a sacred object or deity) the divine couple. Ganesha completed circumambulating the divine couple thrice with full devotion. At the end he claimed that as per the test he went around the world thrice. Though Lord Shiva knew the reason for Ganesha's action, he asked for an explanation from Ganesha as why he did not even start the race to go around the world.

Ganesha replied that Lord Shiva and Parvati are not two different entities and the entire Universe resides in them. Circumambulating the divine couple means going around the entire Universe. So with this Ganesha not only went around the world but has gone around the entire Universe, thrice. Ganesha with his wisdom and quick thinking completed the test in a very less time which no vehicle in creation would have completed so soon. The divine couple were satisfied with the answer of Ganesha and presented a prize in reward for his wisdom.

(Many stories narrate that Ganesha's vehicle is rat and is slow compared to Murugan's Peacock vehicle and this was the reason why Ganesha choose to go around his parents. In fact the rat of Ganesha is also a divine being and can carry mountains on it. It was actually Ganesha's wisdom that made him to understand the true nature of his parents and win the test).

Meanwhile Murugan did not find Ganesha competing with him and wondered he might have given up. After thrice circling the earth, Murugan returned back and saw that Ganesha was already rewarded with the prize. He learnt about the wisdom of Ganesha and accepted that his elder brother deserved the prize. However, he felt little humiliated with his act of going around the world thrice without giving a thought in understanding the reason behind the test by his parents. He was well aware of his abilities as a warrior, but felt he has to grow in knowledge and wisdom. So he decided to leave Mount Kailash and do penance on earth to attain the Supreme knowledge.

Testing Lord Ganesha and Murugan skills

Thus Murugan sacrificed Mount Kailash, the place of Salvation as believed by Shaivites, to attain Supreme knowledge. As per various narrations in various puranas, it appears that Murugan left his family out of humiliation. But there is a reason for his act of descending on earth. Unlike other gods, Murugan descended on earth to bestow his grace on his devotees directly. Many stories related to Murugan happened in and around places near Tamil Nadu. It is believed that even today Murugan appears to his devotees.

10.Phalani

After leaving Mount Kailash, Murugan descended on earth and choose a place to start his meditation. He denounced all his riches and was wearing a white loin cloth holding a spear in hand. For years, Murugan meditated at this place.

The divine couple were missing their younger child and wanted to pay a visit to his son. Lord Shiva and Parvati were happy watching their son. Noticing this Murugan became conscious from his mediation and paid obeisance to his parents. The divine couple requested Murugan to get back to their abode along with them. But Murugan told them that he had to bestow his knowledge and grace on his devotees and he want to achieve this by residing on earth. However, occasionally he would be visiting Mount Kailash to meet his parents. Seeing the selfless sacrifice of their son, the divine couple proudly announced Murugan as their fruit of knowledge - Phalam (meaning fruit in Sanskrit). Since then the place where Murugan was meditating came to be famously known as Phalani. The divine couple blessed Murugan and left the place. Murugan later resumed his meditation.

Years later, Sage Agastya was travelling south (Southern part of India) where he was staying with his wife. He wanted to carry two hills to south to balance the earth as the northern hills were growing tall. The sage appointed a huge demon called Hidumban to carry the two hills. Hidumban was one of the survivor from demon's army in the battle with Tarakasura. After the battle, Hidumban became devotee of Murugan and was wandering in the forests where he met Sage Agastya.

As instructed by the Sage, Hidumban carried two hills on his shoulders with the help of a balance. He followed the Sage to the south. On the way, the Sage decided to take rest. Hidumban placed the balance containing the hills on the ground and took rest. When the two wanted to resume their journey, Hidumban was trying hard to lift the balance. He was not able to even make a move with the balance. He did not understand why he was feeling the balance heavy which was not heavy when he started the journey. He looked at the balance and found a young boy, glowing bright, was seated on top of one of the hill. He ordered the boy to climb down. But the boy rejected. After a tough argument, Hidumban took his sword to slice the boy. The bright boy and the huge demon fought vigorously. In the fight, Hidumban got defeated and was almost got killed by the young boy. Hidumban was exhausted and wounded in the fight.

Hidumban carrying 2 hills on balance

Sage Agastya who was watching this felt that it is very uncommon for young boy to fight a huge demon like Hidumban. With his power of vision, he came to know that the place is Phalani and the boy was none other but Murugan himself. Sage Agastya paid obeisance to Murugan. He requested Murugan to spare the demon, who out of ignorance, fought with the deity he was worshipping. Hidumban too prayed Murugan for forgiveness for his act. Impressed with the devotion of Hidumban, Murugan blessed Hidumban with his original form and asked him to wish for any boons.

Hidumban requested for two boons. First, he should be blessed to guard the hill where Lord Murugan stood before their fight. Secondly, whoever visited Phalini carrying offerings to the Lord in the balance should be blessed like him. The Lord of War granted the boons. Hidumban then placed the hill out of his balance. Murugan returned on top of the hill watching his devotees who seek his blessings. Sage Agastya and Hidumban resumed their journey to South with the hill left in the balance. After placing the hills in the south, Hidumban returned back to

Phalani and resumed the task of guarding the hill in Phalani where Murugan was residing.

11. Son as Father's Teacher

Once Lord Brahma, the creator, visited Mount Kailash to meet Lord Shiva. Young Murugan noticed Lord Brahma and folded his two hands as Namaste to pay obeisance. As Lord Brahma is considered to have knowledge of all vedas (holy scripts), Murugan requested Lord Brahma to discuss on various facts about universe, creation and many more. Lord Brahma was hesitant and showed little interest as he believed that Murugan was too young to understand the secrets of universe. However, they both started discussing about various facts. During their discussion, Murugan asked Lord Brahma to explain the Pranav mantra AUM (ॐ).

Lord Brahma was stunned and remained in silence unable to answer the question. Murugan confronted Lord Brahma for being over pride. An argument arose between Murugan and Lord Brahma. Murugan imprisons Lord Brahma believing he is not worthy to take the tasks of creation. With Lord Brahma being imprisoned, the creation has come to still. There were no births and deaths. The gods were surprised not finding Lord Brahma anywhere. Later the gods learnt that Murugan has imprisoned him. The gods pleaded Murugan to release Lord Brahma, but in vain. They finally approached Lord Shiva to rescue the creation.

Lord Shiva asked Murugan to release Lord Brahma. But the young boy objected saying Lord Brahma was not worthy of his job as he does not know the meaning of AUM which was part of creation. Lord Shiva asked Murugan whether he was aware of the meaning of AUM and asked him to explain about it. Murugan choose a place to explain this where he sat and requested Lord Shiva to sit as well. Here he explained about the meaning, significance and existence of the Pranav mantra AUM. Lord Shiva was very pleased the way his son explained the meaning of AUM along with many interesting facts. He was overwhelmed with joy. Lord Brahma was also impressed and accepted his ignorance. Seeing Lord Brahma feeling guilty, Murugan accepted to release him.

Out of joy Lord Shiva called his son as "Swaminatha Swami" meaning The Teacher of Lord Shiva. Since then the place where Murugan thought Pranav mantra to his father is called Swamimalai. Some stories refer that the Swamimalai hill was the left over hill which Hidumban carried after resuming his journey from Phalani. Years later temples were built around the place by the then ruling kings.

Lord Shiva impressed with Lord Murugan's preachings as Brahma & Vishnu watch them

(As a reference to one of the story, once a sage was performing penance to gain supreme knowledge. To avoid any disturbances, he spell a curse saying anyone who disturbed his penance would lose all his knowledge. The intensity of sage's penance created fires around his body which were consuming the plants and animals in the forest. Years later the penance started tormenting heavens. The gods panicked but did not dare to disturb the sage's penance fearing the curse. They requested Lord Shiva to rescue them. Lord Shiva awakened the sage from his penance and took the curse upon him. Immediately he lost all his knowledge. With Murugan explaining the secrets of universe while explaining Pranav mantra, brought back his knowledge. Thus Murugan removed the curse spelt on his father by imparting his knowledge to him).

12.Marriage with Valli

Murugan was married to Devasena. After he settled on earth, he showered his grace on his female devotee – Valli, who wanted to marry him. Murugan married Valli after several adventures.

Once there lived a man by name Nambi. He was the chief of his tribe in the mountain and was in charge of the welfare of his tribe. He was a great devotee of Murugan, whom the tribe considered as their God of Mountains. He had sons but wished to have a daughter. So, he and his wife were sincerely praying to God of Mountains to bless them with a girl child. One day when he was hunting to gather food, he heard the cry of a baby. He went closer to the child and saw the bewitching beauty of the baby. He brought the child home and began to foster the child as his own daughter. He named her Valli, as he found the child in the creepers on a mountain (Valli means creeper in Sanskrit).

The child grew as a beautiful nymph on earth and was rewarded as the princess of the mountain tribe.

Nambi started his search to find a right match for his daughter who can protect her. Meanwhile, Valli developed a sense of devotion and affection to their family deity who was Murugan. The tribes called him Murugan in their local language. She decided to wed only Murugan and no one else. Murugan was moved by the highest form of love expressed by the mountain princess. So he planned to appease her in person.

One day Nambi sent her to their millet field to protect the crop from dangerous animals and birds. Murugan disguised himself as a handsome hunter as if he had lost his way on chasing a deer during hunting. He approached Valli for guidance and started interacting with her. He later expressed his intension to marry her. Valli who was devoted to Murugan, rejected his proposal. The hunter tried hard to impress her in many ways, but Valli would not listen. Nambi was returning to field after collecting food from hunting. Seeing Nambi, the hunter left the place and turned into a tree to avoid being seen by Nambi and his tribes.

Murugan then took the form of an old man and approached Valli. The old man said that he was very hungry and requested Valli to feed him. Valli gave some grains and honey to the old man. After finishing the meal, the old man said that he was thirsty. She drew water from a pond to quench the thirst of the old man. After satisfying his thirst, the old man asked Valli to satisfy his thirst as a companion. Valli was astonished. She once again rejects the proposal saying she would marry only Murugan and no one else. Unable to do anything, the old man left the place.

Murugan approached his elder brother Ganesh for help. He explained the incidents how he approached Valli and was unsuccessful in appeasing her. Ganesha thought for a moment and decided to help his brother. He explained a plan to Murugan.

Valli as usual went to the field and was watching the crop. Nambi went to the nearby fields to harvest the crops. He would return after the harvest is over. Ganesha took the form of a wild elephant and started chasing her. Valli got scared and started running, screaming for help. She ran for protection and came straight into the arms of an old man who approached her earlier. She pleaded him to save her from the elephant. The old man agreed to protect her, but for one condition. Valli should marry him. Valli didn't had much time to think and agreed to marry the old man and closed her eyes in panic.

The elephant disappeared into the forest. When Valli opened her eyes, she was astonished to find Murugan in the place of old man. Murugan explained about the incidents that took place and revealed his wish to marry her. Valli gave her consent and said that she would marry Murugan in the presence of her father and relatives. They continued enjoying their time in the green fields and beautiful mountains.

Lord Muruga as old man & Lord Ganesha as elephant

When Nambi returned from the harvest, he could not find Valli. Nambi along with his sons and relatives searched for Valli. She was found with an old man on a mountain. Nambi shouted at the old man to release her daughter. The old man rejected. Nambi and his tribe shot numerous arrows at the old man. Not a single arrow could hurt the old man. Instead,

Nambi, his sons and their people fell lifeless on ground as if they were pierced with arrow.

Valli was disheartened to see her family lifeless. She requested Murugan to bring back the dead to life. Murugan instructed her to revive them herself and by her mere touch everyone was brought back to life. Nambi and his tribesmen realized that it was their God of Mountains, in the form of an old man and prayed to him. Murugan took his true form and blessed the tribesmen. Nambi conducted the marriage of his daughter and their God of Mountains. Since then Valli became the second wife of Murugan. The couple lived in the mountains to bless the wishes of his devotees.

Marriage of Lord Murugan with Valli

(Some myths state that Valli was born from a doe when a sage laid eyes on it during a break in his meditation. It is said that Devasena and Valli were daughters of Vishnu born out of the tears of joy of during his incarnation as Trivikrama. They were named Amritavalli and Sundravalli. They expressed their wish to marry Murugan to their father. Vishnu instructed Amritavalli and Sundravalli to perform penance and please Murugan to fulfill their desires. Murugan appeared before them and told that he would marry them when Amritavalli would be born to Daksha and brought up by Indra as his daughter and Sundaravalli would be born to a Sage and brought up by chief of a tribe, Nambi).

Murugan blessing Amritavalli and Sundravalli

13.Saint Arunagiri

During 15th century, a boy by name Arunagiri was born in a town called Thiruvannamalai (in Tamil Nadu). Their family was devotees of Murugan. His father died soon after his birth. His mother and sister instilled him with their cultural and religious traditions. They both loved Arunagiri and wanted to bring him up in rich cultural. After few years his mother too died and he was brought up by his sister. As a kid, Arunagiri showed interest in learning and studied the scriptures. But later as he grew, his interests turned out to be different.

Arunagiri started enjoying the company of prostitutes. Rather than spending time in worshiping gods, he often visited their houses for his pleasures. His sister never objected as she wanted Arunagiri to be happy. Taking advantage of his sister's affection, he took all her jewels and possessions to satisfy his sexual pleasures. Arunagiri was well versed and was good in composing poems. Sometimes, he used to compose poems on Murugan and sell them to rich people to earn money. The money earned was spent to satisfy his pleasures.

As time passed, Arunagiri fell sick very often and developed diseases on his body. He was affected with leprosy and lost all his energy and handsome looks. People started avoiding him as he was diseased and smelt badly. Not learning from his mistakes, he continued with his passions.

One day, as usual Arunagiri demanded money from his sister. This time his sister had no money. Arunagiri shouted at his sister for denying money to him. His sister then said that **he should sell her to someone to get the money**. After hearing these words from his sister, Arunagiri realized about his mistakes as how he wasted his time and energy in satisfying his bodily pleasures. He was depressed and went to Thiruvannamalai temple dedicated to Murugan. He repented for his crimes. Every time he repented, he bagged his head to one of the pillars in the temple, begging for forgiveness. He took a decision to end his life and climbed on top of the temple to commit suicide. Arunagiri prayed to

Murugan with folded hands and jumped from the top of the temple. He fell unconscious during the fall.

Lord Murugan disguised as a Brahman holding Arunagiri

After few minutes, Arunagiri opened his eyes. He didn't feel the pain nor blood stains on his body. He was blinking his eyes and trying hard to open them as golden color brightness surrounded him. From the brightness, he felt as if he was suspended in air held by the hands of a Saviour. A sound emerged from brightness saying *"Arunagiri, you are not born to fall and die. You are born to fulfill divine task to rise and save other lives. You are the chosen one to sing the glory of Lord Murugan"*. As the sound got deeper, the brightness made way for Arunagiri to see who was holding him. It was the divine vision of Lord Murugan. Arunagiri was overwhelmed with emotion seeing the majestic form of Lord Murugan who was dressed divinely, holding his spear, mounting a peacock and radiating bright rays. He folded his hands, paid obeisance to Lord Murugan and sang first devotional song dedicating to the Lord.

Lord Murugan blessed Arunagiri with knowledge and advised him to work on composing poems and spread happiness and knowledge to people through his poems. Since then Arunagiri visited various shrines of Lord Murugan. He travelled various places and spread the greatness of Lord through his beautiful compositions. Wherever he visited, he was blessed with appearance of Lord Murugan as a child or as a young boy dressed majestically. One of his famous work was Tiruppugazh. It had variety of rhythmic pattern of hymns in praise of Lord Murugan. He also composed many devotional songs on Lord Shiva and Parvati.

14.Challenges of a Devotee

Arunagiri gradually developed popularity wherever he went with Lord himself directly blessing him. Few priests were jealous of his popularity and wanted to defame him in public. They asked Arunagiri to face a challenge by a priest on matters of scholarly works. Whoever lost the challenge had to cut off his ears. Arunagiri happily accepted the challenge. The priests and Arunagiri discussed on various scriptures. At the end, the priest lost the challenge. The priest had to pay for insulting Lord's devotee. But Aurnagiri, graciously permitted not to cut off the ears of the priest. Aurnagiri faced similar humiliation in the court of King Devaraya.

King Devaraya had honoured Arunagiri as 'Poet of Royal Court'. The King had a friend called Sambanda who was jealous of Arunagiri. To please and get favor of the King, Sambanda invited Arunagiri to a contest in which he and Arunagiri should each undertake to manifest their deity before the King. It was stressed that whoever failed in the attempt should leave his domain. Arunagiri accepted the proposal as he believed that Lord Murugan would answer to his prayers and manifest Himself in front of the king.

Sambanda first undertook to manifest his personal diety, Goddess Kali. His proceedings were with great pomp and ceremony. Kali did not choose to present. Now it was Arunagiri's turn. He started singing Tiruppugazh appealing to Lord Murugan with complete devotion, pleading to appear and fulfill his prayers. Lord Murugan appeared with His peacock through one of the pillars in the court to bless Arunagiri. The brilliance of the manifestation of Lord Murugan was very bright, equal to hundreds of suns. People in the court were unable to see this with their ordinary eyes. Due to this everybody lost their eyes including the king and ministers. This clearly proves that Arunagiri was an ardent devotee of Lord Murugan. But Sambanda would not learn from this. Sambanda blamed Arunagiri for making them loose their eye sight.

To get back their lost sight, one of the priests asks for jasmine flowers. Sambanda asked Arunagiri to get the jasmine flowers in order to cure the eye sights. Arunagiri secretly transformed himself into a parrot and left his body in the temple to fetch the jasmine flowers. Sambanda learnt about this and burnt Arunagiri's body to stop him entering into his body again. On his return with the jasmine flowers,

Arunagiri could not find his body. Thinking it as grace of God for a purpose, he spent rest of his life as a parrot.

Arunagiri as parrot as Sambanda watch him

Arunagiri was born as a bright boy, but developed bad habits as he grew and finally with mere realization, he became one of the greatest saint and devotees of Lord Murugan. Most of his works are very famous. His poems, songs and challenges changed many lives. He was in one way responsible in restoring balance in human beings by filling their hearts with devotion. In Tamil literature, he is regarded as one of the greatest saints and is famously known as 'Arunagiri Nathar'.

15.Granny Avvai

Long back, there was an old lady called Avvai
(meaning old lady in Tamil language), holding a
walking stick in hand. There is no clear mention of
her original name nor about her birth. Comman
people, especially children called her 'Avvai'
because of her old age. She did not have a family.
However she was a learned scholar and as a result
she had access to Kings Palaces and their courts at
any time. She was devoid of accommodation and
was often traveling southern parts of India.

Avvai was one of the very famous poetess in Tamil literature. As an ardent devotee of Lord Murugan, she always sang songs in praise of Lord. As such, she treated Lord Murugan also as her God in the form of a child. She taught young children on great principles through her sweet little poems. While wandering in villages, she ate whatever meals the people of that village offered her with love.

Once Avvai decided to visit Lord Murugan in Phalani. As she was poor, she could not afford any mode of transportation. So, she decided to walk to reach Phalani. On the way, Avvai had to cross thick forest. She started her journey in the morning. It was almost in the noon that she was struggling hard to walk in the hot sun on a rough path without food and water. On the way she was searching for trees that bear fruits and ponds for water.

At certain distance, she was happy to find a Jambu tree bearing sweet Jambu fruits on it. But the tree was tall and it was difficult for Avvai to pluck the fruits. As she came close to the tree, she saw a young boy sitting on a branch of the Jambu tree. The boy looked bright and gorgeous with an innocent but playful face. She took the village boy to be a shepherd and illiterate. She felt hesitant to ask an illiterate boy for help. But her hunger urged her to request the boy's help to get at least some of those sweet Jambu fruits.

Avvai went close to the tree and asked the boy to pluck her some Jambu fruits. The boy looked down from the tree at Avvai. He asked whether the old lady wanted a warm fruit or a cold fruit. The learned and scholar Avvai was puzzled for a moment. Later she thought the boy was ignorant and illiterate as there would be no warm or cold fruit. It would be just a Jambu fruit. To have fun and tease the boy, Avvai asked the boy for warm fruit. The boy laughed once again and shook a branch of the tree which was full of ripe fruits.

Avvai started to collect the juicy fruits which fell on the ground. She blew air on the fruits to remove any soil particles from the fruits. The boy who was watching this asked Avvai whether the fruits were very hot as she was blowing hard against the fruits. Avvai was astonished to hear these words from a boy. She now understood that the boy was referring the ripe fruits as 'warm fruits' and unripe fruits as 'cold fruits' to tease her.

Avvai felt embarrassed to the fact that she was defeated by an illiterate village boy. With shameful look, Avvai looked at the boy who was not seen on the tree now. Suddenly, bright yellow light flashed in the forest. From the light emerged Lord Murugan seated on a peacock. The Lord said that Avvai was tiered and week to walk in the forest to reach Phalani. So, he helped her fetch something to eat.

The Lord chooses to help her and remind her of values not to evaluate people by their appearance. He then blessed Avvai for a peaceful life and disappeared. Feeling very pleased that her beloved God himself had actually come to assist her and bless her, Avvai sang several songs glorifying Lord Murugan and worshipped the lord with love. Some of her famous works include Vinayagar Agaval, Moothurai.

16.Vadamalaiappa

India was one of the main source of trade in the world economy. During 17th century, India was plundered by many countries. There was war among Portuguese, Dutch, French and British to invade the richness of India. They stole many valuable idols, spices, jewels, etc from India. One such exploit took place in Tiruchendur in Tamil Nadu.

Around 1648 AD, there was war between Dutch and Portuguese to gain authority on India. During this period, the Dutch soldiers took shelter in a temple in Tiruchendur. They want to plunder as much wealth as they can from India. So, the Dutch soldiers planned to escape with Lord Murugan and Nataraja idols in the temple, assuming they were made of gold and vandalized the temple. Since then, the trouble for Dutch soldiers started.

The Dutch soldiers first tried to melt the idol for gold. Their attempt was in vain and the idol did not melt. Unable to melt, they tried carrying away the idol to their country through sea route. But the sea suddenly grew stormy and wilder. The waters rocked the ship violently. The Dutch soldiers understood that this was the wrath of the Gods whose idols they were stealing. The Dutch soldiers immediately threw the idols into the sea. The waters calm down and the Dutch soldiers resumed their journey.

The Tiruchendur temple priest was Vadamalaiyappa who was an ardent devotee of Lord Shiva. He came to know about the theft in the temple and was nervous. He informed about the theft to the king. He requested king to make new idols that resembled the original idols. As requested, the king ordered to make replicates of idols.

When the idols were ready and had to be installed in the temple, Vadamalaiyappa had a dream. In the dream, he was informed about theft and Dutch soldiers dropping the idols into the sea. He was asked to get back the original idols and install in the temple. Instructions were given about the exact location of the idol.

Idol was to be found at the spot where a lime fruit would be found floating and the place is marked by the circling overhead of a bird.

Vadamalaiyappa along with few villagers went into the sea in search of the idols. They followed the instructions from the dream. After several hours of search, Vadamalaiyappa finally recovered the original idol and reinstalled it in the temple in the year 1653.The replicated idols were installed in Tiruppirantisvarar.

Vadamalaiyappa with his devotion and service to gods in the temple brought life and power in the idols. This helped to recover the idols.

17.Pamban Swamy

Not very far from now, in this Kali Yuga*, had a saint called Pamban Swamy. He showed that realizing and receiving grace of Lord Murugan can be achieved by any common man even today. All we need to do is to have faith on our deity and awaken our soul spiritually.

Pamban Swamy was born on 1848 in a Shaivate* family on a Pamban island near Rameshwaram in Tamil Nadu. His original name was Appavu. He showed interest in learning and was good at studies. He developed devotion towards Lord Shiva and lived a spiritual life.

At the age of thirteen, he had a vision asking him to write poems on Lord Murugan. The boy immediately took bath and started writing a poem every day. The poem was ending with Arunagiri's name, whom Appavu accepted as his teacher. He wrote for 100 days finishing 100 poems. People liked the poems of Appavu noticing the devotion in the poems. Gradually his fame spread across Rameshwaram and people compassionately called him Pamban Swamy as he was from Pamban Island.

With the grace of Lord Murugan many miracles took place in Pamban Swamy life. Following are the miracles:

<u>Curing daughter's illness</u> -

Pamban Swamy was married to Kalimuthi and they had a son and two daughters. One night the younger daughter of Pamban Swamy was crying with severe illness. Kalimuthi tried hard to calm the child. But the illness showed no sign of getting cured. Kalimuthi asked Pamban Swamy to apply Vibhuti* on the fore head of child (It was a ritual in olden days to get rid of ill effects by swallowing or applying Vibhuti on a body).

Pamban Swamy insisted Kalimuthi to pray Lord Murugan instead of applying Vibhuti. After this Pamban Swamy was meditating on Lord Murugan. After completing meditation, he noticed that the child had stopped crying and was fast asleep. He enquired about the change in the behavior of the child. Kalimuthi replied that when Pamban Swamy was meditating, a saint visited their home and gave her Vibhuti to apply on the forehead of the child. Soon after that the child stopped crying and got better from illness and fell fast asleep. Pamban

Swamy realized that the saint was none other but Lord Murugan who saved his daughter's life.

Never to visit Phalani –

As a devotee of Lord Murugan, Pamban Swamy visited holy shrines of Lord Murugan whever he got a chance. One day Pamban Swamy's friend was visiting Phalani. Pamban Swamy was eager to visit Phalani and without informing any family member, he left to Phalani. His friend asked whether Pamban Swamy had permission from his Lord to visit Phaani. He lied to his friend that he had consent of Lord Murugan to visit Phalani.

On the same day, Lord Murugan appeared to Pamban Swamy and said that if he wished, Pamban Swamy journey to Phalani could have been easier. He need not lie to visit Phalani. The Lord instructed Pamban Swamy that he would call him to visit Phalani when the time is right and not to visit Phalani till then. To keep his word Pamban Swami never went to Phalani till his last days.

Pair of slippers –

Once Pamban Swami was walking on a rough path. A thorn pricked and pierced into his foot. The pain was unbearable and made Pamban Swami to shed tears. Even in his pain he did not forget to pray Lord Murugan. He felt just by meditating Lord Murugan would make him forget his pain.

On the same night Lord Murugan came in the dream of a cobbler in the village nearby the rough path. The Lord informed him to make and give a pair of slippers to Pamban Swamy. When Pamban Swamy was traveling to the village the next day, the shoemaker came with the pair of slippers to Pamban Swamy saying that in his dreams Lord Murugan came and gave instructions to make a pair of slippers for him. Pamban Swamy was very much pleased and thanked Lord Murugan.

Power of Vibhuti –

Due to his frequent visits to different places to deliver the discourses on Lord murugan, Pamban Swamy once fell very ill due to diarrhea. One day due to severe diarrhea, his body lost all his energy and he fainted. Watching her husband lie on the ground unconscious, Kalimuthi too fainted.

Few minutes later, Lord Murugan came to their home and woke up Kalimuthi. He showed Vibhuti in his palm and asked her to apply it on Pamban Swamy's body. But Kalimuthi was afraid to touch Vibhuti as it was her menstrual time. Lord Murugan said to her that there is provision to women during emergencies. As said by the Lord, Kalimuthi applied Vibhuti on Pamban Swamy's body. Slowly Pamban Swamy got conscious and was later cured of diarrhea. The couple were filled with joy and thanked Lord Murugan.

Journey to a Saintly life –

At the age of 45, Pamban Swamy decided to renounce the material world and become a saint. As a tradition, a person should get invoked with specific hymns by his spiritual teacher to become a saint. Pamban Swamy who accepted Lord Murugan as his teacher was determined to get invoked by his Lord to become a saint. To achieve this he dug a pit in the burial ground and locked it. He started meditating Lord Murugan in the pit without taking food and water.

Once a spirit in the burial ground started troubling Pamban Swamy. But Pamban Swamy chased the spirit by hurling his staff on it. After a week into meditation, he heard divine voice asking him to open his eyes. Pamban Swamy insisted that he would open his eyes only when he see Lord Murugan in the form of Phalani deity. As said Lord

Murugan of Phalani appeared and invoked Pamban Swamy to saintly hood.

Original picture of Pamban Swamy

Black Magic –

As a saint Pamban Swamy was liked by common man. He successfully restored the lost glory of various Shaivite* deities. This was not liked by few priests who always pose a threat and opposed Pamban Swamy's works.

Once these priests tried to kill Pamban Swamy invoking dangerous evil powered demon through black magic. When the demon tried killing Pamban Swamy, he used his yogic power and controlled the demon. He instructed the demon to return back from where it was created. The demon went back to the person and killed him, who invoked it.

Pamban Swamy also filled cases for more than seven years against persons who had published ill of Siva and Saivites. He won every case with the help of Lord Murugan.

<u>Miraculously Cured</u> –

In 1923, Pamban Swamy was injured when a horse cart ran over him in Madras (Chennai). He broke his left ankle and was admitted in a general hospital in Madras. The British doctor said that a surgery was required for the injured leg (India was then ruled by British Empire). Pamban Swamy instructed his disciples to follow the instructions of doctor.

One of his disciple, Chinna Swamy was not liking the surgery to be performed on Pamban Swamy. He had faith in Lord Murugan and believed that Pamban Swamy would be cured if one prays sincerely to Lord Murugan. That night, Chinna Swamy was sincerely reciting Shanmuga Kavacam (wrote by Pamban Swamy) in order to please Lord Murugan to cure Pamban Swamy. Chinna Swamy had a vision of spear entering Pamban Swamy's broken ankle.

Next day, the doctor were making arrangements for surgery. He was surprised to notice that the broken ankle was now in perfect shape and condition. Miraculously, the injury was cured without any surgery. Everyone understood that this was the result of grace of Lord Murugan. Pamban Swamy was kept under observation to get cured completely before his discharge.

On 11th day in hospital, Pamban Swamy had a vision. He saw two peacocks dance before him and Lord Murugan in infant form lying next to his bed. Next day, Pamban Swamy told his disciples to perform Mayuravahana Seva (carrying Lord Murugan on a peacock mount) without fail in Thiruvanmiyur temple. Even today this is celebrated annually in the temple.

Final Journey -

One day Pamban Swamy called Chinna Swamy to look for land in Tiruvanmiyur as his last days were near. The land was dug and arrangements were made for Pamban Swamy to enter into Samadhi state (meditative consciousness).

On 30[th]May 1929, Pamban Swamy called his disciples and advised them to believe in Lord Murugan. Then he took a deep breath and entered Samadhi state.

His works on literature brought common man close to Supreme soul. Pamban Swamy with his teachings and poems won many hearts in Tamil literature.

Dictionary:

Kritika - They are six sisters also known as the six Pleiades, an open star cluster in Indian astrology.

Kali Yuga - The fourth and present age of the world, full of conflict and sin.

Shaivate – Society of people who worship Lord Shiva as their deity.

Vibhuti - Sacred ash which is made of burnt dried wood.

Printed in Poland
by Amazon Fulfillment
Poland Sp. z o.o., Wrocław

53511559R00049